AWAKEN

THE HEALING

OF YOUR SOUL

*Discover your Intuitive Gifts, Connect with your Guides,
Heal your Soul*

AMY J. WINSETT

COPYRIGHT

ISBN 9798522395162
Cover by/Photo by Illustrations copyright © 2021 by Leanne Winsett Noble
Instagram.com/leowinsettartist
Printed in the United States of America
In collaboration with;
Susana Perez from
Creativo Publishing, LLC
www.susanaperez.us

www.serenityenergywellness.com

amywinsett@serenityspautah.com

In loving memory of my brother, Dave.
Thank you for being one of my closest spirit guides.

TABLE OF CONTENTS

Copyright..1

Introduction..7

CHAPTER ONE
Seeking for Answers...11

CHAPTER TWO
The Power of Belief...19

CHAPTER THREE
Intuitive Gifts...25

CHAPTER FOUR
Connecting with Your Guides...33

CHAPTER FIVE
Receiving Messages...41

CHAPTER SIX
Angelic Assistance...49

CHAPTER SEVEN
Recognizing Blocks and Imbalances..................................57

CHAPTER EIGHT
Clarity and Validation...65

CHAPTER NINE

Healing the Soul 71

CHAPTER TEN

Self-Guided Healing Meditations 79

CHAPTER ELEVEN

Continuing the Journey 89

ABOUT THE AUTHOR...91

INTRODUCTION

We live in a time when people are seeking more answers. We are no longer satisfied with believing that what we are seeing and hearing in the physical world is "all that there is." Diseases like anxiety, depression and many others plague our society. Unfortunately, far too few who suffer from these conditions have been able to find lasting relief.

Along with the growing need to find effective healing solutions, there has also been an "awakening" happening throughout the world. For many of us, our egos are finally ready to let go so our conscious minds can connect to a Higher Power. Through this connection we've been able to allow this source of enlightenment to dwell within us. As a result, we have started to notice our own spiritual and intuitive gifts getting stronger and stronger over the last several years.

This new awareness that is emerging has been exciting but has also brought up many questions, especially to those that we often refer to as Empaths. These Empaths have a keen ability to intuitively see things not presented in the physical world. They sense and feel the emotions of others as if it's a part of their own experience. They tend to be our best caregivers and healers. In fact, if you felt drawn to read this book, you are probably one of them!

Deepak Chopra teaches us that "the answers are all within." However, if we don't take the time to learn how to use these intuitive abilities to find those answers, we will miss many opportunities that could bring healing to a world that's hurting.

I've known since I was a child that I was highly intuitive. At the age of eight I started having dreams of buildings and places that I'd never seen or experienced before. Days or weeks later, I would see these places for the first time in the physical world while traveling with my family. These "coincidences" were only the beginning of discovering my intuitive gifts. Many other gifts have developed along the way.

My awareness of these gifts led me to my career as an Intuitive Energy Reader and Energy Wellness Teacher. For the past several years, I have guided hundreds of souls in discovering their own spiritual gifts. Almost daily, I get to take part in the process of helping them clear their own personal, spiritual blocks. My clients consistently report back to me about the miraculous shifts that have taken place in their lives following our sessions. These changes have occurred as a result of them learning how to awaken their spiritual intuition by connecting more closely to the Source of all Healing, God. In doing so, they have naturally and instinctually realized their own healing experiences; knowing exactly what specific prayers were needed for their well-being.

It has become increasingly obvious to me that I need to make this information on how to embrace this pattern of healing available to more than just my one on one clientele. This message needs to be available to everyone seeking it. Thus, I feel I have been led to write this book.

In this book you will learn the skills needed to awaken your ability to see, sense and feel the energetic imbalances in your soul that aren't serving you. As you learn to activate these intuitive gifts, you will be able to hear the divine messages that were meant to guide you on the path to healing.

Your healing is important. Not just for the obvious reasons of wanting to be happy and feel good, but because it allows us to move into a space of creation. This is where we are able to bring about our soul's higher purpose in this journey we call life. You were meant for more than your pain! We must find healing so that we can have the true joy that comes from fulfilling our soul's purpose and creating the life we desire.

Mastering the ability to heal the soul by using your intuitive gifts is a lifelong journey. Every day and every situation provides a new opportunity to learn and grow. However, in my experience, just being on the path to healing feels almost as good as being healed!

Decide today to embark on this journey. Don't allow yourself to waste another minute wondering how to find the answers that are already inside your soul. The journey begins right here, right now!

As you apply the concepts taught in this book you will find peace and enlightenment you didn't know existed. Now is the time to open our spiritual eyes so we can heal our souls and embrace our truest, highest selves.

CHAPTER ONE

SEEKING FOR ANSWERS

How can I become more intuitive? Who are my guides and are they with me? How can I heal from my emotional and spiritual wounds? What is my soul's purpose?

I'll never forget how completely engulfed I was with these questions after teaching at my first Energy Healing Conference (https://www.energyhealingconference.com/) in August 2019. Over 1,400 men and women were in attendance, all of whom were interested in learning about natural and holistic wellness practices. I had taught an Energy Wellness class with a colleague of mine that morning. I spent the rest of the day at my vendor booth interacting with many of the conference attendees. Every one of them had been seeking answers to questions similar to these. I found it nearly impossible to take even the smallest of breaks until the conference had concluded.

Each one of these individuals seemed to be in different and varying stages on their intuitive journey. Each one came to the conference seeking answers according to what their needs were at that time. Perhaps you can relate to their intense desire to learn more.

In general, I found that their search for clarity looked like this:

First, they wanted to learn how to tap into their intuition and discover their own spiritual gifts. Second, they were eager to connect with their guides and loved ones beyond the veil. Third, they were seeking ways to heal from the pains of the past for themselves and their loved ones. Finally, they were seeking inspiration that would provide some clarity as to what their soul's mission was here on the earth.

Phew! That was quite a list. Although these topics seem very different from each other, they actually work in complete harmony with one another. In fact, each of these is the way in which we awaken the healing of our souls!

In general, I have found the awakening process to work like this:

BELIEF ~ INTUITION ~ GUIDANCE

HEALING ~ PURPOSE

Belief: It all begins with the desire to believe. If we don't believe in a Higher Power from which all truth and healing originates, it makes it difficult to fully embrace all that He desires for us to have. We stay stagnant and doomed to keep repeating patterns in our lives that haven't served us. However, if belief is activated or if we have even the smallest desire to believe, we can more fully activate our intuition which allows us to be led along the path of enlightenment and purpose.

Intuition: When we are *in-tune* with our Higher Power, we are able to see and understand higher vibrational things. Thus it is called *in-tuition*. When we are *in-spirit*, we can then be *in-spired*. Our spiritual eye is open and we are ready to receive messages from the other side.

Guidance: You are not alone on this journey! You've been given angelic guides who are there to show you the way and who speak to you through Spirit energy. Your belief and intuition have allowed you to become more sensitive to their messages. They are there whether or not you believe in them or feel like you can hear them. Learning from their messages is crucial to guiding your healing and finding your purpose.

Healing: We all have pain whether it be emotional, physical or any other type. Any pain is a part of a low-vibrational experience. We don't always know what to do with pain or trauma as it happens to us, so we tend to let those low vibrations stay within us. We literally store them in our bodies and spirit, or in other words, our souls. This creates blocks and imbalances in our soul's energy, making it difficult to feel connected to higher vibrational powers. It is evident that we need to find healing in order to clear the pathways that lead us to our soul's purpose.

Purpose: You were meant for more than your pain. While the healing process seems unending, since we are constantly under attack, your journey doesn't end when you are healed. Even just a small amount of healing in some areas of your life can free up energy needed to activate your creative powers. In this healthier state, we feel good and want good things in life. These desires of our hearts are just a part of reading our soul's contract, the things we were meant to do to become higher vibrational beings. Fulfilling your mission FEELS GOOD! It is what will bring us the most peace and joy. It is what gives us that sense of purpose that all human beings are constantly seeking.

Therefore, it makes sense why so many people at the conference that day had so many of the same questions.

Each one was searching for the part of the awakening process they were focused on at that time. Ultimately, they were all wanting to learn more for the purpose of their soul's progression.

The process of awakening begins by first consciously making a connection to your Higher Power, which requires your intuitive gifts to be activated. Without this divine communication, it would be difficult to remember our soul's contract that was written before we were born into these bodies that have no memory of such things. As the spirit and the body become more united in purpose, so does our purpose become more evident. The spirit must first remember, then teach the body. Together, they work symbiotically to accomplish all things spiritual and physical in this mortal realm.

It all begins with believing!

The Awakening Process

BELIEF   **PURPOSE**

INTUITION   **HEALING**

GUIDANCE

What stage of the Awakening Process do you feel you are in right now, in your life? Are you still working on believing or are you ready to discover your intuitive gifts? Have you already connected with your guides and are now ready to hear their messages? Are you feeling like your energy is cleared and healed enough that you're ready to enter into the creation process to fulfill your life's purpose?

You may feel like this process repeats itself. Whenever we go up a level in our progression, it always starts with raising our belief and so on and so on. So if you feel like you're working on raising your belief vibration, that doesn't mean you're at the beginning. Belief is always the beginning of any new idea or journey.

The answer to the following question may feel like it changes from day to day or even moment to moment. Answer intuitively according to how you have been feeling lately.

Which step in the Awakening Process do you feel you are working on right now? Circle one.

Belief   Intuition   Guidance   Healing   Purpose

CHAPTER TWO

THE POWER OF BELIEF

There is a power that comes with belief. That power comes from your Higher Power, which is far greater than yourself. Many refer to this Higher Power as God or Heavenly Father, or Source Energy. He is the source of all love and light and works at the highest vibration. Thus, He is all knowing and can command anything to change, shift or move at will. There is no fight or argument. It just is!

We are here to learn how to match this frequency to the best of our abilities so that we too can have this kind of changing power. Although we are pretty early in the learning process, we do have an amazing opportunity called mortal life to learn, grow and practice. The more we believe in this power, and believe we can become like it, the faster we can learn to grow and shift as He does. This happens especially when we are motivated by the highest of all vibrations, love.

Isn't that an interesting idea: that we are here to become more like our Higher Power and not simply be victims to our circumstances? What would God do if he didn't like something? He'd SHIFT IT! And He *does* shift things all the time! His intent is always motivated by the purest, most incomprehensible amount of love.

As we learn to embrace higher intelligence through love, we begin to think and feel more in alignment with our Higher Power. We spend less time whining about why things are the way they are, instead replacing those feelings with gratitude, even when things don't shift the way we originally thought we wanted them to. Staying connected to this higher vibrational being creates clarity, vision and a deeper understanding of life's challenges. Thus, we no longer feel like victims but active participants who are grateful for the opportunity to learn things from a higher realm.

In a world where it is quickly becoming more common to believe in no other power than yourself or those you see around you, it is understandable that we feel disconnected or unaware that we *can* connect to this source of power and enlightenment.

Take note that the very fact that you are alive is proof that there is a power that nourishes you; the same one you originated from. There may be a growing number of doubters in the world but remember, just because someone doesn't believe something exists or is true, doesn't make it not true!! In order to tap into the power of your intuition and healing, it is essential to believe in a Higher Power who is your Source of Life.

Hopefully, by now, you've discovered that you have a desire to believe in a Higher Power. This desire to believe is enough to set you on the path of your healing journey.

But what if you don't feel you deserve to have this power aid you in your healing? Pay attention to this next part closely: Your connection to your Higher Power has NOTHING to do with deserving!

We often believe that we only *deserve* good things when we *do* good things. Although it helps speed up your progression, by being someone who values high vibrational choices, there is no need to let your lower vibrational choices become your reason to stop believing that this Source is here for you.

Source energy wishes to stay connected to you no matter what, knowing that if it does, you are more likely to want to come into alignment with it and thereby make higher vibrational choices. Remember: it loves you more than you can comprehend. It will never give up on you. Take advantage of this incredible love and remove the false beliefs that are blocking you from it, such as feelings of being undeserving.

Consider the experience I had with one of my clients a few years ago. James came to me one day feeling very frustrated, and even angry, at life. He was missing a loved one that had passed away several years previously and also felt like he wasn't worth much. At the time, he was struggling with feelings of hopelessness but believed that he might be able to find some healing answers through our session.

For about an hour he laid on my table while allowing me to use my intuitive gifts to sense and feel his emotional and spiritual pains. As each different emotion that popped up in his energy field was validated, he began to feel better. Instead of shoving his pains deeper down into his being to be covered up and ignored, we took the time to truly "look" at them and feel them. Since this process requires intuition and inspiration, the natural side effect is the feeling of being inspired or *in-spirit*. In order to be *in-spirit*, your vibrational frequency must be raised to closer to that of your Higher Power.

Wherever there are higher vibrations, the lower vibrations have to leave. Take it from Albert Einstein who said, "Everything is energy and that's all there is to it. Match the frequency of the reality you want, and you cannot help but get that reality. It can be no other way. This is not philosophy. This is physics."

James got up from the table saying, "Wow! I feel so much better!"

But what did he do during that 60 min session to "deserve" those good feelings? All he physically did was lay there. But he believed! That belief opened him up to raising his energetic vibration, which resulted in him gaining a greater sense of wellbeing. Thus, belief is an essential first step in the healing process.

If you believed that you were a victim to nothing and could have whatever you were a vibrational match to, what in your life would you shift right now?

_____

What would you hold in its place instead?

_____

_____

_____

_____

_____

_____

CHAPTER THREE

INTUITIVE GIFTS

W e've all been given spiritual gifts from our Higher Power to help us on our journey. Your intuition, or ability to be *in-tune* with Spirit energy, is one of the most important. While a lot of people have developed their intuitive abilities immensely, many others remain unaware that they possess this ability to see, sense, feel, hear or know things beyond their immediate physical awareness.

We are all intuitive on some level. As we become more aware of those gifts, they will continue to grow, allowing other intuitive and spiritual gifts to also become awakened.

It is often said that "Seeing is believing," but in this case, it is the believing that activates the seeing. Believing is not only seeing, but it's also sensing, feeling, hearing and knowing. I can think of nothing more reassuring to me in my life than the security that has come from being able to connect with deity through the gifts of spiritual intuition.

To better understand these gifts, I have broken them down into the four most common types of intuition. As you read these, think of which ones have come the most naturally to you in your life.

Basic Types of Intuition

Sensing/Feeling: You quite often get a "gut feeling" about situations and things tend to turn out the way you imagined they would. Emotions of others are sensed without them needing to explain them to you. These sensations, usually felt within the body, turn to thoughts that can be processed and communicated through the conscious mind.

You might find it confusing sorting out whose emotions you are feeling, whether they are yours or someone else's. When making decisions in life, it is more important to you that it *feels* right rather than how logical it may seem.

Those who we refer to as Empaths are best described as having the gift to sense and feel. They have the ability to pick up on the subtle energies of others that many easily miss.

Many suffer from anxiety and tend to be more reclusive in social situations in an attempt to protect themselves from these "extra" feelings. Learning to understand their gifts so they can decipher those energies is essential to their own well-being.

Knowing: You don't know how you know, you just know! This type of intuition is commonly found among doctors, nurses and the scholarly, to name a few. The knowing type are the last ones to think of themselves as intuitive. It is such a quick process that it would seem as though the information comes from years of study or knowledge rather than a higher power or intuition. However, the ability to recall information quickly is a form of intuition.

When my friend, Savannah was in her first few months of working as a nurse she encountered a situation with an elderly gentleman who suddenly went code blue (cardiac arrest). In that situation, it was critical that all hospital policies and procedures were implemented exactly as prescribed.

This particular unit of the hospital didn't experience code blues very often because most patients were, in general, fairly healthy. It shocked everyone who was working there, leaving them scrambling to figure out what to do. However, to Savannah's surprise, she just knew what needed to be done.

She was one of the only ones in that critical moment who seemed to remember all the procedures that needed to be taken. She checked his vitals and started CPR, all while telling the other nurses, who were more experienced than her, what they needed to do. The other nurses were in awe of this newer nurse's ability to react so quickly and accurately in this critical moment.

My friend explained that she knew from the beginning that the man wasn't going to make it. After all, she is highly intuitive in several different ways. However, the hospital's lifesaving procedures still needed to be implemented. She said, "Somehow I just knew what to do!"

This is an excellent example of the intuitive gift of knowing. It wasn't just her training that helped her perform her duties: after all, the other nurses had been trained the same way and had more years of experience. This was an affirmation of her ability to know because she is a highly intuitive being.

Hearing: The gift of hearing is not limited to what you hear with your physical ears. More often, you may feel certain subtle vibrations in the ears that give off the *feeling* that you're hearing certain sounds or messages. For instance, it might *feel* like you're hearing people cheering, singing or crying. Or perhaps you have an impression of other sounds like birds chirping or a train whistle blowing. These sounds may only be heard, in that moment, through the spirit energy of your ears.

The following story is an example of how sounds from the spiritual realm came through to the physical world in order to validate the presence of my client's loved one.

Amber had come to see me several times previously, but on this particular occasion we sensed her grandmother's presence especially strongly. She was very close to her grandmother before her passing. She had shared with me that her grandmother loved hummingbirds, which is why she had a tattoo of one on her arm.

A few minutes later, I heard the sound of wind chimes coming from the area just to the left of my client's shoulder. I said to her," Did you hear that? I just heard wind chimes!" She said, "Yes, my grandmother loved wind chimes!"

I had wondered if it had come through on my music playlist, but I have heard that playlist many times before and since and there are zero wind chimes on it. We asked others outside our room if they had heard anything and none of them had a clue what we were talking about. For me, this was certainly an unusual experience. For some of you though, this might be a more regular occurrence if you have been given the intuitive gift of hearing.

Seeing: If this is your gift, you might describe yourself as being quite "visual". Seeing types are often vivid dreamers at night. You may frequently see flashes of light in the corner of your eye or, at times, a dark shadow moving swiftly past. Perhaps a loved one has appeared to you before from beyond the veil.

While seeing things in the physical world from the spiritual world is a part of this gift, it is not limited to just what the physical eyes see. Most of us will utilize this gift through the use of our spiritual eye only. Information will come to you much like it does in a dream, but during meditation in the waking hours. Colors of light and images will come into the mind's eye, but may not necessarily show up in the physical world.

If that is the only way you ever see energy, rest assured that that is enough. After all, belief is what brings about the seeing in the first place, whether it be in the physical or spiritual world. It is not necessary to see with the physical eyes in order to get the messages needed for your healing and spiritual growth.

My dear friend Megan has the intuitive gift to actually see Spirit energy with her physical eyes. However, it is not always a positive experience. She has seen some negative things and entities that would scare the pants off of most of us, but there has been a positive side to her gift of seeing as well.

Over a decade ago while going through some really tough trials in her life, she saw the spirits of a little girl and boy. She felt, through inspiration, that they would become her future children someday and that she should hold on to hope. She has since birthed them both and they are now 12 and 10 years old. There were many other times that she would tell me she could see her late grandmother watching over her from the corner of her living room.

Which of these four types of intuition best resonates with you? Have you had different gifts activated at different times according to need? Just starting to recognize the ways in which you've already been experiencing intuition will activate your gifts further.

No one is stuck in any one of these types alone. As long as you are staying open to the possibilities, you will see them shift, change and grow. It's an exciting process and it is happening more quickly than ever before as our world continues to go through an Awakening.

Discovering your intuitive gifts will give you the confidence you need to hear the messages available to you for your healing. You'll be able to connect more powerfully with your loved ones, special guides and angels that eagerly await the opportunity to assist you.

Number your intuitive gifts from 1 to 4. 1 being your strongest gift and 4 being your least. Remembering that as you strengthen one gift it will start to spill over into other gifts as well.

____Sensing/Feeling ____Knowing ____Seeing ____Hearing

CHAPTER FOUR

CONNECTING WITH
YOUR GUIDES

One of my favorite things to do when I teach an Energy Wellness class is to demonstrate how to use the hands to intuitively read energy in the body. During one of my presentations, in a class of over a hundred participants, I asked for a volunteer to demonstrate this technique with. About 15 individuals immediately raised their hands. I felt drawn to call on a woman in the back of the classroom whose hand I saw go up the fastest.

As I began to connect with her energy to read where her energy blocks or imbalances might be, I could only feel one thing. She had a male spirit energy with her that day. This special spirit came through with a loving, fatherly energy. When I asked if her father had passed, she said he had. I told her that I could sense him there and that he was eager to communicate with her that day. She said she could feel him too and began to tear up.

I then continued to read her energy for the purpose of the demonstration, but first told her to come see me after the class so we could discuss more privately what I had been feeling about her dad.

Later that day she explained that she wasn't sure how her hand had shot up so fast. She had no intention of coming up to the front to have everyone stare at her and put her out of her comfort zone. She said, "Somehow my hand just shot up there. I was completely surprised to see my own arm raised!"

This woman had been going through a difficult relationship breakup. She had been desperately seeking for support and answers in her life. There is no doubt in my mind that it was her father that lifted her hand for her so that she could receive the comforting reassurance that she was not alone in her struggles.

Your angelic guides and loved ones beyond the veil are there for you too. You are never alone. So why then do we seem to struggle with knowing how to connect with them? Shouldn't we already be feeling them if they are always there anyway? Well, yes, and no.

Spirit energy works at a higher vibration than we do in the physical realm. Even though they are always near, you might not be sensing them or able to clearly hear their messages. The closer you're able to bring your vibration in alignment with theirs, the more connected you'll feel to them. You'll be able to hear their messages better and more frequently notice the signs they're showing you.

If raising your vibration to that level feels impossible, do not despair. These angels also lower their vibration enough so we meet them somewhere in the middle. These spirit energies are subtle and most of the time nothing is going to smack you on the head to let you know they're there. If you keep staying open and believing, you'll begin to notice the evidence of their presence more and more.

Take a minute to imagine that you are surrounded by guides and angels that love you. Perhaps let them sit in a chair next to you. Allow your mind to be freed from worldly cares for at least a couple of minutes. Then get ready to receive information from your angels, even if all you hear or feel is a one-word message.

While searching through YouTube a few years ago for videos about intuitive energy experts, I stumbled across a video of a woman who was a Medium, meaning she has the gift to connect with souls on the other side and receive their messages.

In the video, she demonstrated the following technique on a friend. She explained that if you'd like to connect with your personal guides, a loved one, etc., then you could do the following.

She told her friend to choose someone from the other side of the veil that she wanted to connect with. Her friend chose her own mother.

The medium told her to let her mind go completely blank for a few seconds to a minute. She explained that the first object to appear in her mind's eye would be the very object that would appear in the physical world within the next 24-48 hours, validating that her mother was near.

As her friend did this, she said the object that came to her mind was a boxing glove. This left her feeling discouraged, thinking that she wouldn't see a boxing glove show up in the physical world in the next day or so. She figured this little exercise probably wouldn't work for her.

A few hours later, the two of them were riding on a bus headed into town. A passenger sitting behind her friend had dropped their keys, which then slid under the seat where she was sitting. As she bent over to pick them up to give back to the passenger, she was astonished to see that one of the keychains on this set of keys was a miniature boxing glove!

She looked at the medium in total surprise. She knew through this simple, sweet validation that her mother was with her.

I was fascinated by this new technique I had stumbled upon and tried it for myself. I was interested to know if my angel guides were with me. I cleared my mind and then allowed an object to appear. I saw an empty casserole dish. I thought it was odd, and proceeded to go about my day.

Almost 24 hours later, I heard a knock at my front door. A neighbor of mine was returning dishes to those of us who had brought meals over to a different neighbor who'd been sick from cancer treatments.

She had an 8 x 11-inch glass dish in her hands and asked if it was mine. I said "No, I brought some lasagna to them in a glass pie plate." At this point, she was frazzled from knocking on so many doors in the neighborhood just to figure out who this dish belonged to.

She didn't know anything about my pie plate so she shoved the glass dish into my hands and said, "Here, take this then!" I said, "Cool! I always wanted a smaller casserole dish like this. In fact, I'd have used this instead of a pie plate had I owned one!"

It wasn't until about two or three hours later that I realized what had just happened. I thought, "Oh my gosh!! A casserole dish just showed up at my door! It worked! My guides *are* with me!!!

Fast forward to now... Of course I know my guides are with me and of course her friend's mother is with her. Since then, I've become incredibly acquainted with spirits beyond the veil in many different capacities. I found this to be a fun way to get the ball rolling!

Try this exercise for yourself:

- Choose someone you'd like to connect with that's beyond the veil.
- Clear your mind for up to a minute.
- Allow an object to appear in your mind's eye.
- Wait 24-48 hours (typically) for that object to appear in the physical world.
- When it shows up, be sure to say a prayer of thanks to your loved one or guides and Higher Power.

I'd like to connect with

_____

_____

The object that came to my mind was

_____

_____

Journal your experiences once your object that represents your loved one or guide has manifested itself.

CHAPTER FIVE

RECEIVING MESSAGES

Now that you understand how to connect with your guides and loved ones, it's time to start recognizing their messages. Sometimes, these messages are simple and are only meant to validate that your loved one is near. Other times, we are seeking clarity on bigger issues and the messages may be more profound.

There are many ways in which we come to be aware of angelic messages. These are some of the most common and recognizable ways they may come through:

Thoughts: The simplest and most frequent way of hearing their messages is in your own thoughts. It's also the least recognized way we receive guidance from them because we usually just think our thoughts are exactly that, *our* thoughts. You might be pretty surprised if you actually knew how many of those great ideas that have popped in your head have actually been given to you by inspiration through Spirit energy.

Friends and Family: Ever have the experience where you're talking to your mom about a problem you're having and she offers some advice? You then tell your best friend the same thing and she offers the same random advice. Then, perhaps, on to a third person. You can thank your angels for speaking through them to try to get a message to you. Be sure to pay attention to such coincidences. And, by the way, there are no coincidences!

Imagery: A lot of times, during meditation, you'll notice various images coming through that seem to have little to do with the problem you're seeking answers for. Alternately, you might notice certain objects appearing at an unusual rate in physical form in the conscious world. However these images may be manifesting themselves to you, there is a way to interpret their symbolic meaning.

I love using an app called Dream Moods (http://www.dreammoods.com/dreamapp.htm). While it is meant to help you interpret the dreams you have in your sleep, it is also useful for understanding the meaning of signs coming from the subconscious mind during meditation or appearing repeatedly in your waking world.

Whether awake or asleep, these images may be your angels trying to communicate with you. When you look up the meaning of these images in this app or one similar, use your intuition to help you know which part of the interpretation is meant specifically for you. Angels love using objects and images. They know you can look up its meaning and find a whole paragraph (or more) of information interpreting their messages. All they had to do was get your attention long enough for you to notice one little object.

Numbers: If you've been noticing that you always seem to look at the clock at the same time every day (ex. 3:33) or a certain pattern of numbers keep showing up for you (ex. 123), it might be your angels sending you a message. This same app, Dream Moods, will interpret a lot of the numbers you're seeing, too. I also have a book called Angel Numbers 101 by Doreen Virtue that makes it easy to look up number meanings. Watch out specifically for the number 11, 111, 1111 and so on because 11 is the sign that your angels are watching over you and guiding you. You are on the right track!

Always use wisdom and intuition when interpreting number meanings. Numbers aren't meant to be the only way to know if you're on the right track in life, but they usually serve as a second confirmation to something you've already decided. If you're open to noticing numbers, then the angels will use them to communicate with you from time to time. If numbers aren't your thing, no worries. The angels will find other ways to send you messages.

Don't drive yourself crazy trying to pay attention to every sign or symbol. There is no need to act desperate for these messages. Pay attention when you get the feeling that this is something you should pay attention to, especially when you notice certain images or numbers that keep repeating themselves.

Journaling: Some people are very good at writing down their thoughts and feelings on a regular basis… and then there's the rest of us. I do not journal as often as I could, but when I am truly seeking guidance about something, I pull out the pen and paper. It is such an easy and powerful way to capture the inspirations you're meant to have for your soul's progression.

Begin by opening your journal to a blank page with pen in hand and start writing whatever comes to mind. The more specific you are about what you're seeking answers to, the better. If nothing comes to mind, write "nothing." Sometimes, we need to validate that the issue is a lack of knowing. Afterwards, ask, "What's next after *nothing?*" and keep writing.

Journaling can work in the other direction as well. If there are things you know you want help with from the other side, then write them down. The angels love it when we make lists! You'll be amazed at how they take that information and run with it simply because you became clear on your desires and intentions and wrote them down.

Meditation: To be in a state of meditation, you must allow your mind to be freed from your daily stress and thought patterns. In this space, information can flow freely from the subconscious mind to the conscious mind. Sometimes, you'll be in this space for only moments at a time. Other times, you may choose to stay in it longer, according to your needs.

The number one thing to do when meditating is to find a quiet space. Go for a walk in nature or lie down on your bed. Sit in a special place in your living room or go for a drive to get away from distractions. Ever notice how many good ideas have come to you in the shower? Our best "ah ha moments" come when our minds are freed from distractions.

Meditation is a skill that takes practice, just like developing your ability to read, write or ride a bike. In chapter 10 you'll learn how to do some Self-Guided Healing Meditations. As you consistently use these meditations, as well as others, you will strengthen your ability to get into this quiet space in the mind where you can tap into information stored in the deeper parts of your subconscious.

Prayer: Most of us are familiar with some form of prayer. It is a way to communicate directly with God, our Higher Power, through our quiet thoughts or by speaking them out loud. While too often it seems it's just us talking to Him, nothing could be further from the truth. Prayer is actually a two-way exchange of information.

I had a beloved friend, who has now passed, that I often referred to as my "spirit guide in the flesh." We talked almost daily for years while she was still alive. She would often say to me, after I'd finished complaining about some aspect of my life, "What answer did you receive when you prayed about it?"

More than a decade ago, I thought that it was completely acceptable to not hear anything right away after pleading to God for answers to my problems. In contrast, she expected to hear answers immediately and taught me to do the same.

If I was going to complain to her about a problem in my life, I knew to pray about it first, and then listen for an answer. I didn't want to come up empty handed when she, once again, asked, "What answer did you receive when you prayed about it?" I've learned that there is *always* an answer that can be heard, even if it's just a little one.

The process of receiving these messages is not meant to be very complex, nor is it meant to be difficult to understand. Most of the time, they are simply trying to point out the stuff you might be missing. These messages are there to remind you of your soul's purpose and give you the direction you need to stay in alignment with your Higher Power.

For example, for the last several years, I have felt inspired to write a book. I've known for quite some time that I would need help and guidance in the process. A few months ago, at the age of 42, I mentioned to a client of mine that I'd probably write my first book when I was 44 years old. I felt my guides quickly correct me saying, "No, you'll be 43!" So here I am, at the age 43, making it happen. I hired my book coach, Susana Perez (susanaperez.us) to guide me through the process and there you have it! Writing this book has been a part of fulfilling my soul's purpose.

As you become more aware of the messages that are there to guide you, you'll experience a greater feeling of purpose in your life. Stay open and be positive. Then, get ready for information that will come from your subconscious mind into your conscious mind.

Take a few minutes to think about some images or numbers that may have been showing up for you lately. Look up their meaning in the Dream Moods app or in a similar resource. Numbers meanings can also be looked up on the internet by searching for *Angel number meaning*. Write your answers below.

An image I've been noticing a lot lately_____

The image meaning that best resonated with me

_____

Numbers that keep appearing in my life

_____

Number meaning or message

_____

CHAPTER SIX

ANGELIC ASSISTANCE

One day, during a session, my client, Olivia, asked me if I could see any angels around her. As I searched for answers in the angelic realm, I could see that she had many, many angels. Legions of angels, in fact! I told her they were standing all around her and her husband, home and children. She said, "I pray for angels *all* the time!"

I was curious as to what these angels, that she'd prayed for so regularly, had been doing for her. I wanted to know in what ways they were specifically blessing her life. When I looked again, I could still see them but I didn't get a clear impression of their exact mission. So I said to her, "Do you ask these angels to do anything for you?" She said, "Umm… No, I guess not. I just pray for them to be near me and my family."

This led us to discuss a very important part of the process of asking for assistance from angels and guides. We often pray for angelic beings to surround us, but we don't think to ask them to do anything specific for us. Or, at least, not specific enough.

Don't get me wrong... it's awesome that she had so many angels in her life. That is some really high vibrational stuff! But they were capable of doing so much more for her. It is our job to ask for what we need and not assume that they'll just go ahead and do it. It's not that they don't want to help you, but, according to the law of the higher realm, they must receive permission from you to do so first.

It doesn't always need to be a specific verbal prayer, though. In fact, just an inkling of the heart is enough for them to be able to act upon. However, you must first decide what you want.

Imagine going to a restaurant to order food and having a conversation like this with the server:

You: I'm hungry.

Server: Well, we have a lot of options on our menu. What would you like to eat?

You: I don't know... something yummy.

Server: Hmm…we *do* have lots of yummy food. What are you in the mood for?

You: I'm not sure…

Server: (waits patiently)

And so on and so on…..

We all know that it is not the server's responsibility to decide how to meet our dietary needs nor choose how much money we are willing to spend. He is willing to serve you, but is waiting for you to figure out for yourself what it is you really want or need. The more specific the better.

Likewise, your angels want to fulfill your needs and desires as fast as they can. When we ask for a little, they help us a little. If we ask for a lot, they will be there for us every step of the way!

There are many different types of angels available to us. Some of them are your loved ones that have passed on. We tend to trust the energy of someone we knew in this life more readily than a less recognizable spirit energy. Others may be ancestors you never knew. Spirit children are often nearby. Several other types of angels are there for you at all times. There are far too many to name.

When seeking angelic assistance, try asking for an expert in the topic you need guidance in. For example, if you need help finding a job, ask for an Employment angel to guide you. If you need to get your car fixed and want to find someone who is honest and reliable, ask for a Car Repair angel. If you are ill, ask for a Healing angel.

Not too long ago, I was struggling daily to get my toddler to let me brush his teeth. He didn't enjoy the experience and put up a lot of resistance. He refused to open his mouth, so I would have to force it open to get the tooth brush in there. I finally decided to pray for a Teeth Brushing angel. The next time I tried to brush his teeth, he happily opened his mouth and I was able to easily complete the task. I've had almost no teeth brushing issues with him since. He is now three years old and even likes to "brush teeth!" by himself.

Angels are there to help with the little things in life like teeth brushing just as much as they are there for the bigger stuff.

I grew up as a military kid and therefore moved around a lot. Many times, I watched my parents use prayer and inspiration to find a home that was right for us. Even as an adult, I've had to call upon Housing angels more times than I'd care to admit. Consequently, when clients tell me that they're stressed out about finding a place to live, I suggest they do the same thing I advised the following client to do.

Lila came to me one day feeling pretty hopeless about her current living situation. She had left an abusive marriage and was currently living in a women's shelter. She knew she'd need to leave soon, but after weeks of desperate searching she hadn't found a place within her budget that fit her family's needs.

This was the perfect opportunity to teach her about asking for Housing Angels. I asked her to get really specific about the things she, in her heart, truly desired from her new house. I am sure, in her desperation, she probably didn't think her list should be overly specific, but these were the things that she truly desired in a new home, so she began to list them.

First, she knew she needed three bedrooms, two bathrooms, to be close to her children's current schools and to be under $1100 a month in payments. She went on to add that she'd like to have a fireplace, a fenced yard for her dogs, a jetted tub, a stainless steel fridge with a pull out freezer on the bottom, and a workspace for her home business. She also wanted a place she could eventually buy without having to relocate her family once again.

I then asked her to invite Housing angels into her life to guide her to this perfect home. As she did, we both felt the energy in the room shift. I knew her guides would help her find what she needed, but even I was shocked to hear just how perfectly they had fulfilled her request.

Not only did she find a home that had everything she *needed*, but it also had everything she *wanted* - everything from the fireplace to the work space for her business! Everything she had listed, both the necessities and her desires, were fulfilled. Not only that, but the owners of the home accepted $1100 a month in rent until they graciously sold it to her, a year and half later, for $10K less than its appraised value!!

If that doesn't make you want to get specific about your needs and wants, then I don't know what will. There is so much help for us on the other side if we are willing to take the chance, dream a little, get clear on what we desire, and ask for their assistance.

The next time you need or want something, try asking for that particular type of angel to assist you. Keep in mind that the more specific you are, the better!

What kind of angel do you need?

I need a/an _____**Angel.**

What do you want them to do for you? Be as specific as possible.

I'd like my angels to _____.

CHAPTER SEVEN

RECOGNIZING BLOCKS AND IMBALANCES

Angels not only help us fulfill our personal desires, but they also make excellent guides when it comes to discovering our soul's blocks and imbalances. Where there is an *im-balance* there is a *dis-ease*. A dis-ease is anything that makes you feel less than whole, such as emotional, physical or mental pain or discomfort. These dis-eases are trying to tell us that there is something in our soul's energy that isn't serving us.

Believe it or not, your body is perfect and has never made a mistake! Any pain or discomfort you have felt has just been a message from your spirit, speaking through your body, to get your attention so you can recognize your emotional, physical or mental imbalances. When we take the time to listen to the messages that our bodies are giving us, we will not only feel better in the short run, but we can also avoid bigger problems down the road. Your body will die eventually, no matter what, so it makes sense that the messages it's sending us through physical discomforts are for the purpose of healing the spirit energy of the soul, which lives on forever.

What is a Block?

Your body feels best when its energy is flowing exactly as it should. When the Breath of Life, or Source Energy moves freely through your body, it is able to nourish and replenish you. Blocks in our energy occur when there is a restriction to that flow. You will feel stuck or stagnant.

What is an Imbalance?

When the right amount of energy flow is supporting each part of your body, not too much or too little, you feel balanced. When you are balanced there is a feeling of well-being. An Imbalance occurs when something throws the energy off. There may be too much energy being stored in one area of the body or too little in another. This will result in you feeling "off" or unwell.

Where do they come from?

Since *everything* is energy, it's possible that *anything* could affect the wellbeing of your spirit and body, or, in other words, your soul. The most important, but often overlooked, type of energy to pay attention to is your thoughts.

Thoughts are powerful! They have vibrations that send signals to your body, which in turn gives you messages according to the type of thought energy you're holding onto. If your thoughts or core beliefs serve you, then you will feel well, but if they don't serve you, then you will feel some sort of dis-ease which will create a block or imbalance in your energy flow.

How do I recognize them?

You have seven main energy centers in your body. In Sanskrit, an Ancient Indian language, they are called Chakras, meaning the Wheels of Life. These energy wheels spin and draw in energy to keep the spiritual, mental, emotional and physical health of the body in balance. Each of these energy centers resonates at the frequency of one of the colors of the rainbow. Certain thoughts and beliefs will show up in these chakras according to their assigned meanings.

When there are false beliefs being stored inside these wheels of energy, they can become sluggish, change in color and be blocked. These blocks are imbalances which create dis-ease.

For instance, your thoughts and beliefs about your safety will generally show up in your Root chakra. If you feel safe, the energy will move as it should, which feels good. If you are holding onto thoughts and beliefs that make you feel fearful, you will have a disruption in the flow of your Root chakra's energy. Since the root chakra flows from the base of the spine down through the legs and feet, this is also where your physical pain or discomforts may show up.

This chart illustrates the name and location of the seven main chakras, the colors associated with them, and their meanings. Use this chart to guide you in figuring out what beliefs are not serving you based on where you are currently feeling pain in your own body. Do you have a sore throat? Does your stomach feel sick? Read what functions each area holds and try to figure out what false beliefs you may be holding in them.

The 7 Main Chakras/Wheels of Life

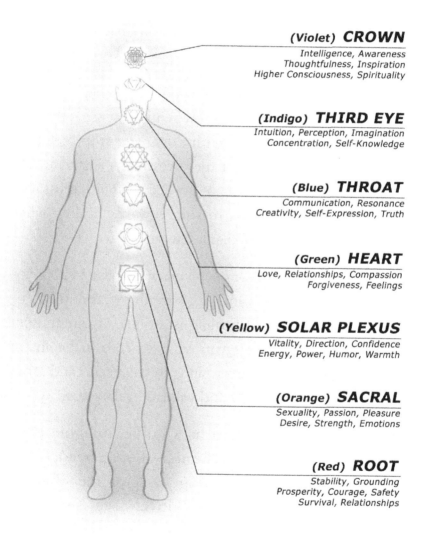

(Violet) CROWN
Intelligence, Awareness
Thoughtfulness, Inspiration
Higher Consciousness, Spirituality

(Indigo) THIRD EYE
Intuition, Perception, Imagination
Concentration, Self-Knowledge

(Blue) THROAT
Communication, Resonance
Creativity, Self-Expression, Truth

(Green) HEART
Love, Relationships, Compassion
Forgiveness, Feelings

(Yellow) SOLAR PLEXUS
Vitality, Direction, Confidence
Energy, Power, Humor, Warmth

(Orange) SACRAL
Sexuality, Passion, Pleasure
Desire, Strength, Emotions

(Red) ROOT
Stability, Grounding
Prosperity, Courage, Safety
Survival, Relationships

Once your conscious mind gets the message that your spirit energy has been trying to teach you through your physical, spiritual or emotional discomforts, your body will be ready to let it go and you will begin to feel well again.

It can be uncomfortable discovering what's causing imbalances in your energy. When we sense our own grief, we often want to shut it down and stop feeling it. We reject the first sign of these emotions surfacing and don't listen long enough to hear their messages. However, energy begins to shift towards healing when we focus on it for even just a few seconds.

Don't be afraid to look deeply at what false beliefs you are storing in your energy. Negativity and pain are limited. The power of healing is infinite. It can and will heal when it has been given what it needs. It begins by recognizing your blocks and imbalances, and then offering them the clarity and validation they need.

Using the Chakra Chart as a guide, imagine there is a light moving from the top of your head, down through your feet scanning each of the chakras. Allow your third eye to intuitively see, sense and feel the messages the energy of your body is telling you.

Which chakra feels the most blocked or sluggish? Draw an arrow pointing to the chakra that feels the weakest right now.

Which chakra feels the brightest and most free flowing? Draw a circle around the chakra that feels the most balanced right now.

CHAPTER EIGHT

CLARITY AND VALIDATION

Once you've discovered where the blocks and imbalances are, it's time to offer them some clarity and validation. It's no wonder that the energy of your soul loves validation. After all, it practically screams at you if you ignore it!

When your energy is imbalanced, you'll get the message in an uncomfortable way. You'll feel sick, tired, panicked, depressed or a myriad of other ailments. The sooner you give your energy the validation it needs, the more comfortable the experience will be.

Don't think that you can ignore what's going on in your soul's energy. You are only fooling yourself. When something inside you doesn't serve your higher purpose, it can't stay quiet. Give it the attention it needs so you can experience the healing that is sure to follow.

Clarity

Sometimes, it will seem like everything inside you is screaming at you all at once. It's like you're at a really loud concert and you can't hear what the person standing right next to you is saying. The information is there, but you can't understand it because there is too much else going on simultaneously.

A place of chaos is not a place of healing. Begin by asking the energy to calm down and get quiet. Then, tell the messages trying to come through to line up in order of importance. Don't question the order. Your angel guides know exactly what order you should address your issues in. Just stay open.

To find clarity, in this case, means to clearly recognize the messages. The first thing that needs to happen is to set the intention that the information will be calm and organized. Use a journal to write things down to help organize the information as it comes to you.

Validation

Have you ever felt left out at a party or other social gathering? Most of us have experienced this at least once. It feels pretty awful. Sometimes, all it takes is one friendly person to help you feel included.

No one wants to be ignored and neither do the messages from your soul. Your energy loves attention. It wants to be seen. Looking at it with your third eye is the same thing as shining a light in the dark. Darkness cannot exist in the same space as light. The light will always win. When we recognize what needs help or attention, rather than ignoring it or burying it, we will naturally, instinctively, and intuitively begin to remedy it.

Next, let the energy tell its story. You may not like the story, but that's all the more reason to look at it and listen to it. There may be memories that pop up that seem old and unrelated. Listen anyways. Pay attention to what feelings and emotions begin to surface as you focus on the messages.

In the book *Feelings Buried Alive Never Die* by Karol Truman, in the section "Probable Feelings Causing Illness," you can look up your physical ailments and learn what emotions or false beliefs you may be holding onto that cause them. I have been using that book as a healing resource for over 30 years. You'll be amazed how accurately it pinpoints the exact feelings that are associated with certain diseases.

Get ready to be surprised by the answers that you find. If the answers were obvious, you wouldn't need to be looking so deeply in the first place. Have confidence that you are not wrong about these messages. If it crosses your mind, then it must be something that needs to be seen, heard and validated.

Choose an area of the body that, from the exercise in the last chapter, you know needs healing. It's time to ask some clarifying questions so you can validate the information that is being held in there.

Does it need to tell a story?

_____

_____

_____

_____

What images come to mind?

_____

_____

_____

What emotions come up?

Does the energy feel stuck or heavy?

Does it feel old and ready to let go?

_____

_____

_____

_____

_____

What beliefs are being held there that don't serve you?

_____

_____

_____

_____

CHAPTER NINE

HEALING THE SOUL

At this point, we have discussed several different steps in the Awakening Process. By now, you have:

- Acknowledged your belief in a higher power
- Discovered your intuitive gifts
- Connected with your angels and guides
- Received angelic messages and assistance
- Recognized your blocks and imbalances
- Clarified and validated your dis-eases

Now, you're ready to...

- Shift what is no longer serving you and replace it with incredible healing energy!

This is such an exciting place to be! Your awakening journey has most likely been rewarding and healing already. You've learned new skills that you can take with you into any situation. You are starting to understand how being on the path to healing can feel almost as good as being healed!

To heal means to make sound or healthy again. That includes alleviating distress or anguish. In short, healing is to take something that doesn't feel good and replace it with something that *does* feel good. It sounds so simple, but we all know how overwhelming that task has seemed to us in the past.

We are under constant attack physically, mentally, emotionally and spiritually. The key is to combat your enemies before they attack. Even if the damage has already been done, there is always a way back to being whole and well again.

To take something that *doesn't* feel good and replace it with something that *does* sounds a lot like the fulfillment people find in addiction. No wonder addictions run rampant in our society! When emotions or pains surface that are unpleasant, people too often run to food, drugs, sex, alcohol, or a myriad of other things. For a short while, they feel some relief from their pain but no actual healing has occurred. In fact, we know that they have only made their pain worse in the long run by ignoring and masking those messages they were receiving.

Addiction almost always creates more pain for the ones they love, too.

True healing feels better than any addiction or any other short-lived attempt at masking our pains and discomforts. Yes, it can be a very painful process to look directly at what is hurting our souls. Hang in there! When you know how big or awful the pain is, that is when you also know exactly how much love and light is needed to remedy it. I have personally seen and felt my pains and the pains of others go away completely after focusing on them for just a few, very uncomfortable, seconds or minutes.

Remember, your pain is limited. The healing power available to you as a gift from your Higher Power is *infinite*!

Envisioning

The final step in the healing process begins with envisioning what you *do* want to feel. You've already recognized and validated what you *don't* want to be feeling. Now it's time to use your imagination so you can understand, and replicate, what it would feel like to be whole again. Doing this does *not* make you delusional. Your mind believes whatever you tell it and your soul's energy will vibrate at the frequency of that thought.

It works like this: What you think, is what you feel... What you feel, is what you vibrate... What you vibrate, is what you attract. It's time to think thoughts of wellness so you can feel well and be well!

Always envision your body and spirit as being whole, even when it seems like they're very broken. The broken parts are just layers that have shown up from hurtful life experiences. As you peel away these layers and uncover your truest self underneath it all, it will feel like remembering someone who is whole, rather than discovering someone new.

Holding and Replacing

The most important part of the healing process is learning to hold a space for the good energy that you've imagined and envisioned. It's a place for the positive vibrations that are replacing the negative ones, to go.

It's a lot like cleaning out your closet. Imagine that you're getting rid of the clothes you no longer need or want because some are far too outdated, smell bad or never looked good on you in the first place. Now that they're gone, there is free space in your closet for what you do want. You'll gradually replace your old wardrobe that was robbing you of the much needed space, with a new one; one that brings you joy!

Create some space in your energy to hold what you do want to think, feel and vibrate. Replace the negative thoughts and feelings with new, positive ones. Tell a different story in your energy than the one that has attracted so much pain to you previously.

Sometimes, this may feel like you're telling yourself a lie, but if you want it to be your truth, say it anyway. It will become your vibrational truth soon enough.

My client, Donna, learned this first hand after a powerful session a couple years ago. I could sense, while reading the energy in her sacral chakra, that she lacked positive mother energies in her life.

She explained that her birth mother had given her up for adoption, her adoptive mother was unkind and indifferent to her, her step-mother was no better and she struggled to have a positive relationship with her mother-in-law.

Anyone would be able to understand how this would make her feel pretty disconnected from positive mother energy. In this case, it would seem natural for anyone to hold negative vibrations in the Sacral chakra, which is connected to feelings of being nurtured and motherly relationships.

I connected with Donna's angels to better know what was needed for her healing. I felt compelled to tell her that, in spite of the fact that she had no earthly mothers of her own to feel nurtured by, she could still experience healing by holding onto good mother energy. I felt instructed to have her think of Mary, the mother of Jesus, and hold the feelings that thought came with in her Sacral chakra. She immediately lifted her arm, showing me a bracelet she had been wearing that had Mother Mary on it. I had not noticed it on her wrist before this discussion. She said she had no idea why she felt like buying it, just a couple of weeks previous to our session, but she had. I believe her guides had been preparing her for this part of her healing.

Donna agreed to practice believing she had good mother energy in her soul, even though it had not shown up yet in her reality.

A couple months later, she found a way to reconnect with her birth mother. As it turns out, her biological mom is a fabulous and loving human being. They regularly spend time with each other, and she's even met her half siblings who have also been a huge blessing to her life. The joy she's found in these relationships has been incredibly healing to her soul.

It's important to hold a space for what we want and need, and then vibrate at the frequency of the reality of those desires as if we already have them. They *will* eventually show up as a part of our reality.

Shielding and Protecting

Once you've been able to create the space for your healing and replace it with higher vibrations, it is time to shield and protect it. To do this, envision a large bubble of light all around you. You get to decide what qualifications are needed before anything or anyone is allowed to enter into your shielded space. If it doesn't meet your demands or respect your boundaries, then it cannot enter in.

Then, pray for angels to stand in a circle surrounding and protecting you from anything that would lower your vibration. This is especially important after a deep healing session has occurred. Sometimes, we need to incubate as part of the healing process. The protective circle allows us the space to do so.

In this next chapter, you will put into practice the process of clearing, balancing, shielding and protecting through three different Self-Guided Healing Meditations.

What is something in your life that you thought couldn't be healed because your reality hasn't provided proof that it exists for you?

_____

_____

_____

_____

Now, hold the energy of what you want in that area of your soul, both body and spirit. Allow your energy to vibrate at the frequency of the gift you wish to have or how you wish to feel; Record how it feels to have those healing vibrations. As those blessings become a reality, be sure to journal your experiences.

CHAPTER TEN

SELF-GUIDED HEALING MEDITATIONS

Meditation is a place you allow your mind to go to. Finding your way into this space is essential to discovering the answers to your spiritual and physical healing. You don't have to spend a long time in meditation in order for it to be effective or "eye opening." In fact, you can get into the space of meditation very quickly once you have developed the skill.

The more you practice meditating, the more you'll be able to connect to the space where all the answers to your soul are kept. Sometimes, you may only need to visit for a few seconds, while at other times you'll want to stay in a deeper state of meditation while pondering life's bigger questions.

While learning this skill, it is more important to focus on frequency rather than duration. At first, you may feel like you can only disconnect your thoughts from the conscious world for just a few seconds, but with time and practice you will be able to meditate for longer periods, allowing yourself to connect to the subconscious mind where you will have some of your greatest "Ah-ha" moments!

Stay positive as you learn to strengthen your ability to meditate. It's common to feel like you're too busy or simply don't have the time. Our fast-paced world is not conducive to the state of meditation.

If we don't take the time to listen to the subtle messages of our souls, we will find that those messages will come out louder in other ways through our bodies. Ways which we will not like. The body will then take the time it needs to heal, usually at some of the most inconvenient times. It's far better to take time to listen now, while the messages are still quiet, rather than waiting for them to loudly strike when you least expect it.

Meditation does take time and practice, but it's worth it! It requires slowing down, breathing deeply, and freeing your mind of your daily stresses. You will find blissful serenity each day as you learn to utilize this beautiful and powerful self-healing technique.

Some form of meditation should happen daily, but it doesn't always need to take up a lot of your time. Here are three very simple, yet wonderful, ways to meditate. They range in duration from a few seconds to an hour. Depending on your day or energy needs, you will want to choose the session length that best supports you. As always, allow your intuition to guide you.

Quick Check-In Meditation (15 -30 seconds)

- While standing or sitting, close your eyes and take one deep, cleansing breath in through the nose and then out through the mouth.

- Using your spiritual eye, bring your attention to each of the seven chakras or energy centers of your body. Start at the root chakra and work your way up to the crown or start at the crown and work your way down to the root.

- Only spend a couple of seconds on each chakra looking to find just one or two areas in the body/spirit that need the most healing in that moment.

- Allow any thoughts or images to come to your mind that are important for validating your soul's messages.

- Take in another deep breath, sending healing energy into the areas you noticed needed the most support.

- Thank your energy for its messages and promise your energy that you'll be open to giving it what it needs throughout the day.

- Finish the session by envisioning a shield of light surrounding and protecting you.

Energy Renewing Meditation (5 -10 minutes)

- Begin by choosing one of your favorite essential oils and rub a couple of drops into your hands. Lemongrass, lavender and frankincense are excellent oils for energy healing.

- Breathe in the aroma of the oil through your nose as you bring your hands close to your face. The essential oils will help raise your vibration so that you can more quickly get in tune to receive messages and clear what's not serving you.

- Lie or sit in a comfortable position with the palms of your hands facing upwards.

- Close your eyes and take three more deep breaths in through the nose and out through the mouth.

- Using your spiritual eye, bring your attention to the top of your head where the crown chakra is located.

- Spend 30 to 90 seconds on each of the seven chakras or energy centers starting at the crown and ending with the root, listening for any messages that they may have for you.
- Notice anything in each area that feels like it's moving sluggishly, looks dark or feels dis-eased.
- Thank your energy for showing you what you saw or noticed.
- Breathe in life to each area that seems distressed.
- Revisit each chakra, imagining that each energy center is swirling and moving freely at a speed that serves you.
- Think of each of the chakra colors corresponding to that specific chakra, offering it the frequency of light that it needs to feel whole and perfect. (Crown- Violet, Third Eye- Indigo, Throat- Blue, Heart – Green, Solar Plexus – Yellow, Sacral – Orange, Root – Red)
- Ask for anything that may be anywhere in your body that is no longer serving you to be released. Imagine that as the darkness releases from you it turns into beautiful crystals of light.
- Breathe in and out deeply three more times before opening your eyes and returning to the present.

- Finish the session by envisioning a shield of light surrounding and protecting you.

Deep Energy Healing Meditation (30 -60 minutes)

- Before you begin, have quiet, relaxing music playing in the background.
- Choose one of your favorite essential oils and rub a couple of drops into your hands. Lemongrass, lavender and frankincense are excellent oils for energy healing.
- Breathe in the aroma of the oil through your nose as you bring your hands close to your face. The essential oils will help raise your vibration so that you can more quickly get in tune to receive messages and clear what's not serving you.
- Lie or sit in a comfortable position with the palms of your hands facing upwards.
- Close your eyes and take in three more deep cleansing breaths in through the nose and out through the mouth.
- Invite your guides and angels to be there to support you and guide you through your session. Wait to feel their presence before moving on with the meditation.

- Using your spiritual eye, bring your attention to the top of your head where the crown chakra is located.

- Place one or both hands on top of your head or allow them to hover two inches above your head. Sensing with your hands the energy that is rising from your body.

- Using your spiritual eye and intuition, starting at the crown chakra and ending with the root chakra, listen for any messages, feelings, sensations or vibrations that may be coming from them.

- Spend as much or as little time you feel you need to read the messages coming from each of the seven chakras or energy centers. There is no need to rush.

- Notice anything in each area that feels like it's moving sluggishly, looks dark or feels dis-eased.

- Take the time to listen to the energy if it needs to tell a story. Be aware of emotions that may surface that have been trapped. This is just a time to look and listen remembering that seeing is halfway to healing.

- Thank your energy for showing you what you saw or noticed.

- Invite Healing angels to surround you and comfort you. Feel the support they are offering you from the other side.

- Breathe in life to each area that seems distressed.

- Hold a positive thought or image so as to feed and nourish your energy with what it was lacking. Listen to your guides and intuition for the answers.

- Revisit each chakra imagining that each energy center is swirling and moving freely at a speed that serves you while also imagining each of the chakra colors respective to each chakra offering it the frequency of light it needs to be balanced. (Crown- Violet, Third Eye- Indigo, Throat- Blue, Heart – Green, Solar Plexus – Yellow, Sacral – Orange, Root – Red)

- Ask for anything that may be anywhere in your body that is no longer serving you to be released. Imagining that as the darkness releases from you it turns into beautiful crystals of light.

- Breathe in and out deeply three more times before opening your eyes and coming back to being present in the room.

- Finish the session by envisioning a shield of light surrounding and protecting you.

A Few Tips:

The more you practice these and other meditation routines, the better you will get at it. You will learn to be guided by your intuition and you will not need to be reminded of each of these steps listed above. Practice, practice, practice!

There are some fantastic guided meditations available on YouTube. Many have specific themes according to the issue it focuses on, such as grief, anxiety, depression, etc. Meditations guided by Bellaruth Naperstack or Jason Stephenson are my favorites.

To find the right kind of music for your self-guided healing meditations, do a google search for *spa, relaxation music* etc.

To purchase good quality and affordable essential oils visit www.myessentialcollection.com. Their frankincense is especially wonderful and far less expensive than most other brands.

Lastly, remember to enjoy the healing journey you are on. It should feel good and be something you look forward to doing!

CHAPTER ELEVEN

CONTINUING THE JOURNEY

By now you're hopefully feeling pretty confident in your ability to find the healing you need to continue your journey and fulfill your soul's purpose. Knowing what we were meant to be, or what our purpose is, has a lot to do with listening to what our hearts are truly desiring. If you want it, you were meant to have it.

Start by asking yourself what you want next time you're wondering what you should do. Be sure that your desires are motivated by love and light. If they are, then you can move forward and have confidence in your decisions. Take comfort knowing that your angels and guides will redirect you when you get off track.

I truly feel that it is a large part of my soul's mission to continue to teach others how to find spiritual peace and wellness. I have spent 20-30 hours a week for the past several years helping others find the answers to some of their greatest life questions. I know, better than most that it takes a lot of time, practice and training to know how to fine tune the gifts we've been given. If you are wanting to continue your energy wellness journey with me, then here are a few powerful resources for you:

Classes and Workshops: I teach affordable classes and workshops regularly so you can consistently learn new concepts and apply them in your life. You'll find the information on all upcoming Serenity Energy Wellness Classes and Events – Virtual and/or In-person at www.serenityenergywellness.com or on Facebook at www.facebook.com/serenityenergywellness

Private Sessions and Spa Services: If you'd like to book a private session with me, or receive a spa service from one of our talented service providers, please book online with us at Serenity Wellness Spa in Kaysville, Utah www.serenityspautah.com or on Facebook at www.facebook.com/serenityspautah.com

Energy Healing Conferences: To hear myself and many other gifted energy wellness teachers speak at an upcoming Energy Healing Conference – Virtual and In-person please go to www.energyhealingconference.com for more information.

ABOUT THE AUTHOR

Amy J. Winsett, author of *Awakening the Healing of Your Soul*

Amy Winsett is an Intuitive Energy Reader and Energy Wellness Teacher in Kaysville, Utah. She grew up as a military child traveling to many places in the world which gave her a broad perspective of the uniqueness of each individual.

She is an extrovert and lover of all people. She has been a performer of music and dance since the age of three. Her ability to express herself through the performing arts has also grown into a passion for teaching others.

She has assisted hundreds of people in discovering their own intuitive gifts, connecting with their angels and guides and to find healing by clearing personal blocks. To be able to share with others how to tap into their own spiritual gifts has been one of her most rewarding experiences.

Amy believes that living true to your higher-self comes from acknowledging your greatest personal desires. When asked what her hobbies are you might be surprised to learn that it's also what she does for a living. Life is to be enjoyed so why not let your hobbies be your source of income.

Amy teaches that understanding how to heal your soul by using your intuition is not just for those "born with the gift," but something we are ALL meant to learn!

She is a mother to five beautiful children and step-mother to three incredibly loving step-children. Her husband's unwavering support has been priceless. Whenever possible you'll find her spending time with family including her parents that live nearby.

She teaches virtual and in-person Energy Wellness Classes and offers a variety of spa services in Kaysville, Utah. She can be found teaching at Energy Healing Conferences hosted by Hope Haven Events in various locations.

www.serenityenergywellness.com
www.serenityspautah.com
www.energyhealingconference.com

Made in the USA
Coppell, TX
19 June 2021

57745980R00056